SALT AND ASHES

SALT
AND
ASHES

ADRIENNE DROBNIES

Adrienne Drobnies

Signature
EDITIONS

Editor: Garry Thomas Morse
Cover design by Doowah Design.
Photo of Adrienne Drobnies by Armelle Troussard.

This book was printed on Ancient Forest Friendly paper.
Printed and bound in Canada by Marquis Book Printing.

We acknowledge the support of The Canada Council for the Arts and the Manitoba Arts Council for our publishing program.

Library and Archives Canada Cataloguing in Publication

Title: Salt and ashes / Adrienne Drobnies.
Names: Drobnies, Adrienne, author.
Description: Poems.
Identifiers: Canadiana 20190057408 | ISBN 9781773240480 (softcover)
Classification: LCC PS8607.R62 S25 2019 | DDC C811/.6—dc23

Signature Editions
P.O. Box 206, RPO Corydon, Winnipeg, Manitoba, R3M 3S7
www.signature-editions.com

for Ariel

I

II

Randonnées

III

I

Witch Hazel Song

Red Rover come over and show me
the games you learned as a child.
How to wield scissors with a vengeance,
how to spank a cat, beat your brother's
head against a wooden bench.
How to be invisible and how not to be.
A shoe hits a face. A slap stings.
Crank up the wind inside you and wind it down.
Red Rover, your burns heal slowly
and scorpions hide under blankets.
The taste of soap in your mouth
empties your insides –
vomit is mopped up with bleach.
A wooden floor smacks the chin.
Splinters are painfully pulled. Car doors slam.
Show me how scars last on ring fingers,
ice burns as much as fire, and *I don't know*
how she got those welts. Teach me the rules
you learned as a child and how a switch cut
from witch hazel is a lesson in pain and power.

It's a blue day

and the goddess of the year has not been kind

The full moon in March is worth being wary of

Remember it was the dog who sniffed Odysseus out

not the child
not the mate

A woman won't wait
Why should she?

I wonder
where was I
and how old
when Joanne Kyger
born the same year
as my mother
sailed between
San Francisco
and Japan

I – a small child –
beaten, shredding curtains
with a vengeance

watched the Kennedy assassinations –
the first one when I was in California
the second in Texas

find myself in another place

menacing hospitality
no man to scowl away the suitors

The Sacred Yew

My old aunt Myrtle
            harder than
                        the hard wood of her name
Any noun can be verbed she said
            and set the table for dinner
                        green print tablecloth and blue plastic glasses
Grandma Bech's everyday china and art deco wedding silver
            acrid smell of polish under my nails

I climbed the crêpe myrtle
            a child shrouded in its leaves
came face to face with the hard-eyed cicada
            scrambled down
                                    not returning
            for weeks
                        Years later the insect is just a specimen
in biology class – with organs
            large enough to see

Taxus tree
            made to bow and bend
yields a poison drug
            from the botanical trash heap
            of mould and groaning wood
for the canker that moans in the flesh

Ring Dance

It's possible we once danced
by the light of the solstice moon,
runcible drunk, hunched over
streetcar tracks to flatten a penny –
the only coin we had to offer
against a thundering weight.
We don't know whether passion
will be renewed at the same address
where ceiling plaster sprinkled our hair
like crumbly feta, garnish to the salt stink
of pleasure. Can we count on postal carriers
to negotiate a contract for delivery of nothing
but billets-doux and arrangements
for assignations at sea? Will the local library
lend us its volumes on love so thigh to thigh
we can sit down again to read instructions
for how to fill an empty vessel?
Will we flip to the page with the pop-up mast
and lash ourselves to it, each siren to the other?
However demented we become, the moon will
shift its light all night on the water
and twist itself into rings we bought
for one flattened penny.

Gold Mountain Miniature

One month into a pregnancy she
wears a cheongsam
cut from beige silk recently
brought back from China.

From the same trip she returns with an
antique coat – black silk lined in sky blue.
She never would have bought it except at his urging
because she thought
it too beautiful and too costly.

There is a word for *crust*
but why is there no single word in English
as there is in French
for the white part of the bread – *la mie*?

Like the word *lining* –
blue that shelters the skin
from a rough-cut exterior.

Was there some clue in the cramped room
where she slipped her hands through the sleeves
this would be the garment she would put on
to listen to a poem he wrote for her
and he would not be there
when she heard it read?

Stanford Hospital, 1987

This is a serious business, says my husband –
a home birth – he will have none of it.
The labour coach attempts a simile –
It's like running a marathon with a broken foot –
though that will come later and bear no resemblance.

My father attempts to be helpful –
I just hope you don't go crazy after the birth
the way your mother did.
No, he is sure, it was your birth that unhinged her.

I am surprised to wake in the night
folding and refolding infant clothes,
a nest fabricated from printed cotton squares.

Wallpaper scenes from
the temperate rainforest,
chosen to soothe in this desert,
where I shift from room to room.

After a week in intensive care
she is fine, but I hold her tightly,
run from the hospital like a fugitive
from the unstoppable fact
I have given birth to this breath,
this child, this life,
this death.

Boiling the lamb shank for Passover

I can use that lamb shank
I say at the French restaurant
and ask for the leftovers.

This is not the place to ask for carry-out –
disapproval arrives with the delivery,
the shank in foil and a brown paper bag.

Pesach still a month off,
remnants are left on the bone.
I boil away the remaining flesh.
Marrow oozes into the broth.
Lamb vapours fill the kitchen.
I set the shank aside, frozen
until the appointed sunset
and candle lighting.

Herders marked their doors
with animal sacrifice
to reprieve their own human cargo
but had no mercy for those left behind.

Yahweh throws his ultimate weight around,
spares not even the firstborn of the slave girl.
No need to mention only sons were slaughtered,
felled as lambs. Girls didn't matter –
not enough wailing.

I have a daughter.
Keep her well under the Abrahamic radar,
safe from the plague in that apocryphal tale,
the one that finally did the Egyptians in,
and I'll boil until day's end.

Perhaps if my own life had been cleaner

I pushed her in front of the car – her death was quick.

Painless – I don't know.
Is death ever painless for being efficient?

Perhaps if my own life had been cleaner.

One morning my mother told my brother and me
to stay in bed until she came back.
She didn't return for three days.
We comforted each other as best we could
but we were hungry.
We ate the only thing in the house – a bottle of ketchup –
red like blood, sticky-sweet, nourishing.
We felt better afterwards.

Bread was the consecrated Texas dust.

She did come back –
didn't say where she'd been.
When I asked her she laughed and said *visiting*.

What shamed me was the way I scarred –
my skin formed ugly welts.

Later, I married.
Married women didn't have abortions.

I killed my girl. It wasn't hard to do.

The hard thing
was giving birth to her.

Dream Poem

A woman and I are walking up a hill

We've been climbing that hill
for thirty years

During this time
our children have grown
and learned to evade us

I tell her I care about her

She does not say what is true:
she does not care about me

The only reason she
travels up this hill with me
is we're neighbours
who share a dislike
of our husbands

We reach the top

look out over a plain
of palms and pines
ibises tall as trees

The Depresso Experience

Those people are just rubbing themselves raw
                    for nothing

you said of the habitués at the cafe
where I had an espresso each morning

safe there among the too earnest

your love like cigarette
        smoke at the back of my throat

slightly stale, mildly addictive
        quietly lethal

No, you say

Now you sit in front of a house
you lived in more than 50 years ago

Now you touch the AstroTurf
that burns your hand

Now you and I and we
from that time are talking

Now you say we lived in the same
sort of suburban rancher

But far away and why a rancher
there were no ranches to speak of

There were fathers and
professors, the old and the dead

And now you live in a new place
that is the same again

Now you say
it is time we walked to the ocean

Among the broken bottles of Hoboken

The stones that fell from Deucalion's hands were men
and those that fell from his wife's hands were women.
—Ovid
The Metamorphoses

Amid these trashy remains
is a way to raise up children

Our mythologies
and our technologies
abound with parthenogenesis

A machine
of crepe de Chine
will chew
the junkyard shards

compress an automobile
frame into a flute
to give shape to human breath

The flesh is
a sounding board
guts are strings

Bones knock against
each another
hinged and unhinged
on a pivot in time

The Devil

Más sabe el diablo por viejo que por diablo

At 22, you mugged my life
arm around its neck
rifling gnarled hands
through its pockets

Pancho Villa's men
invaded the family home
and killed your grandfather
I have paid for those robberies

Was I wrong to hold on to my life?

You yanked it away and
left it twisted with a limp
on its right side

Love, family, career
I would reassemble these
from pieces scattered on the ground

You taught me a valuable lesson
The devil knows more because he is old
than because he is the devil

Looking Back

The Canaanite plains are awash –
the desiccated veins engorged.
Sulfurous green ribbons
in the vermilion hills,
parched as a match, are
once more seasonally quenched.
Steam rises from a bloody mud.

The law is ancient –
to rid himself of
a middle-aged wife
and replace her
with a younger
more vivid version,
sentiment is set aside.

The wife a transparent
memory with obsidian eyes
at which he does not look,
or looks through,
when looking back.

Cloud Mountain

The male deer crosses in front of me on the forest path

      His mate waits
                        until I am safely past

         Rain on the far sheltering roof

Croak of a frog

Into the woods the startled flap of a heron

Two Rottweilers who would tear me apart

if they could learn to cooperate
        and find a way

         over the fence

    quieten against
               my receding back

The sun shines in the rain but no bow

Sign scrawled in red paint
Trespassers will be shot
This is America

Red purple of Japanese maple
             Water flowing from rocks

    Crack of gunshot

          It is hunting season and I am wearing green

Reading to the snow geese

the dead are notoriously hard to satisfy
　　　　　　　　　　　—Jack Spicer

Flying black and white against the sky
the shadow side made light by wave break
beneath their hearts beating too fast
to make wise choices about where to land
They look like paper – an origami design
dressed up in a costume of the real

They shear the wind on the hunt for
Buddha, Lao Tse, and Hermes Trismegistus
They get shooed off the altar all the time
because it is sacred but where then
should they put their feet?

And if the flying dead are not sacred
and scared then who is?

Unwelcome Guest

Coiled creature
I have travelled a long way
to poke you with a stick
and milk your fangs

I move around you
with familiar ease –
the frozen block of venom
you offer as host digests me

I want
        to be a good guest
            not to cause pain
those I love sleep here too

consumed by the knowledge
death is one thing
        life another

Kingfisher

I am the keeper of waters
of calm days and
burning surfaces

My drowning face
my dawning life
my love revived

glints in the water
red poppy
white poppy
Two tangled flames

Seven or
fourteen
Halcyon
days

Write backwards
on the water
a bird flickers
the waves
Green flux
blue flux

Backed into the rain
forest I hear
a howling –
Do not leave home
it says

If you go
you will lose
all memory

Go and you
will lose every
thing

The lion in the earth

The work of the mother lion
is not to rebuke her daughters.

She does not sink her teeth
into their *nuques*
or crack open the sea
with the chant of a manatee
to harvest whale flukes.

The earth made fertile
with spills of grain
erupts with colour

whenever she whispers
of the white rain
and blue stars.

Stars flung down
from a scribbling sky
tattoo her
overarching belly.

The Last Days

C'est tellement mystérieux, le pays des larmes.
          —Antoine de Saint-Exupéry

I lie on the floor and
listen to the gapped breath –
read aloud from *The Little Prince*
feed you spoonfuls of
vichyssoise and watermelon
nibble at the remaining bites

I wear a black silk blouse and
the long flowered skirt
you gave me from Nepenthe
and caress myself
with your knowledge and love
your hands now absent from me

I kneel with three other women
as the space between breaths lengthens

Alone once more
with the stars and soft night
a breeze brushes by
startles me

The day grows light
with the blue of summer
I wash and oil your body
to know one last time every centimetre,
every dimension, every crevice

touch the cold of your forehead
all your knowing still there

Because anger and bitterness are gone
I can write now of the last days
and not be mad with grief

Far from home

But you were beautiful like the interpretation of ancient books.
—Yehuda Amichai

You were my home and I miss you
in a thousand fonts
in serif and sans serif
in Garamond in Calibri in Calisto
I miss you in the remembrance
of things past and the search for lost time
in the embrace of the morning
and the herald of the evening
in the scribble of lightning
above my skylight and the attendant rain
I miss the mark and master quark
I miss you in haiku and sonnet
in alexandrine and pantoum
Your bent words –
May all my Whitmans be Christ
I miss you in kanji and pinyin
in hiragana and Hebrew and hieroglyphics
I miss you in Greek and in Mayan
You were my home and I miss you

Home before dark

Then

there is a shifting
in the leaves
my grandmother recognized –
something stalking her

Hot and hungry
both she
and the animal
afraid but she
bears the dryness
in the mouth
less well

Stock still
in her homemade cotton
dress she makes her way
as silently as she can
through the piney woods
flat pointed shoes
leaving deer tracks
in the dust

Human animals
the ones she feared most
Could be nothing
but a legend –
the black cougar
called panther –
but everyone knows
why a child
sometimes disappears
into the evening
and does not return

Seeing one said to be a bad omen
and she reckoned it true

Tall and willowy
she awaits the spine-severing
strike – the same clean blow
she has used to slaughter chickens

Would her brothers
shoot the animal
with flashes of light
in its eyes
after they planted
her gutted body
in the ground?

She walks a little faster
The rustle keeps pace
Almost home

and now...

in a dream leather jackets
chase me around the gas station
one of them holding a broken bottle
a light bulb hanging from a chain
a fence and a car coming at me
      Don't jump over the fence

Months later I walk past
the Shell station on Alcatraz Ave
Oakland at 2 am
a jogger grabs me around the neck
      Don't say anything

Two weeks before the policewoman
said at the self-defence class
Sometimes a woman's best defence
is just a good scream –
practise in your car
I did

Time slows
unsure if I can
I turn my head
and scream

Heads peer out
from windows
Oh shit
the predator hisses
and runs off

I'm home late
with a head full of rage
but I don't phone the police

Modern Poetry

Easy enough
to assign depression
to the modern condition
declare the numbing
effect of accumulated
losses a recent invention

Sheer toil
kept the brains
of earlier generations
from wallowing
in affluent torpor

tilling the soil
to tend the garden
with the memory
of being exiled
from paradise

White Phosphorus

The Segovia Café, Toronto

Mussels on the menu
Sangria on the tongue
The hot and cold
we plunge into our mouths

Rodrigo said when you die
you become pure music

We never saw the gardens of Aranjuez
and neither did he

Volterra, Italy

I scream down the monastery halls at midnight

No idea what's Italian
for *my husband is diabetic*

I am a semi-Jewish girl
begging the Virgin for intercession

The next morning
the light knocks me back
windows thrown open to a room
you could develop film in

You pick with curiosity
at the tabs on your chest
from electrical leads

The paramedics in the square joke with you

Insentience is hilarious
when you live

Ravenna, Italy

Light drains through alabaster ripple
Towers lean
Streets run the other way

San Vitale racked and buried
alive with stones on his head

Justinian and Theodora
glitter and doze

Dante in exile went underground
to write *The Inferno*
Florence would be a bonfire of himself

The Paradiso in Ravenna
The Underground came in
'44 –'45 and his ashes carried below
safe from bombs

as your infant self
was sent to shelter
in the French countryside
from Nazi occupation

Damn them for white phosphorus in the Vercors
damn them for Jean Moulin
damn them

And you
dead at 56

Vancouver

Landing
I thought
this is the place
I will die
But not you
I did not think you

II

Randonnées

The word *randonnées* in French refers to long walks or rambles.
There is a network of walking trails that extends
throughout France, which is known as
Les Grandes Randonnées.

Grenoble

I. Dans le quartier

June

The place does not matter much
nor how I arrived
nor how I leave.

Leaving
leaving
arriving

among this stand of trees
in midday
domesticity
and the well-practised arts.

I live in the quarter of chemists –
Lavoisier, Gay-Lussac, Berthelot –
who watched walnut oil turn rancid
for eight months and ten days.

As thunder rolls through the mountains –
it is easy to settle here
not to move

difficult to find a trajectory
through the crowd.

The given and the random
are where I begin.

II. Dans le quartier

Stones in my shoes and the sound of wind in spade leaves.
Wet on a summer evening; the vine still at rest
and honey for sale.

Flat, white tiles curve around the brasserie.

I slow down to see a Rose of Sharon–dotted pyramid
a tree in a well.

                    Fingers of willow, fir, fingers
of fern.

III. Sur la montagne

Sweat, sweat, sweat up the mountain.

What is the word for path – *sentier*?
I remember only *piste* – trail.

What is the difference between trail and path?
A trail is more directed – harder-won, harder worn.

A path meanders.

In and out of the regional museum, I wander
past the closed gates of houses:
stiff, upright, iron.

In the haze below rests home.

I pluck wild oregano from the stairs.

A slow rhythm takes hold – the cautious intimacy
of middle age, where much needs still to be said, and it is still
necessary to say it.

IV. Dans le quartier

I am drawn to the yellow-white bitterness of
green plums to assuage nausea.
Succumb to shakes on the constructed landscape
of pyramid and trough.

A buttery woman reclines on the moulded hill,
her leather sack open, book retrieved.

        The air descends – warm displacing cool –
                     soft and continuous.

The woman's dress flaps and curls under the bike
she steers around a curved ramp.
I am reminded of one woman's desire to be beaten.

V. *July*

Prelude and postlude to washing the floor:
things must be done –

rearranging mind and room.

That is where Nerval now walks over the concrete bridge by
Crédit Agricole.

Two advance too close –
below, hiving around a car.

The post hastens to meet my approach
the trees aslant.

VI. Sur la montagne et dans le quartier

August

Not every place is abandoned.
The elements remain, and I am here
with one of them.

Every outward place quickly
becomes intimate and inward.
Every inward place
outward in the
fast-approaching landscape.

Tales rob us of what we see
who we are.

Shimmers hold on in the
dimming light shot upward.

Tales take each word for granite.

My upper lip is a salt lick.
My hand swipes the cool film
around each breast.
Fat hangs there like a butcher's display.
I carry the unwilling sister who
would not go far on her own.

A hard-honed knowing
tautens in thigh
muscles.

Hands tear at flowers
teeth bite the dust.

VII. Dans le quartier

Twilight comes in season.
A shot of blood orange
streaks from the Dent de Crolles –
ragged tooth.
Rag and bone
tooth and bone.
The green turns blue.

I am aligned with the white
panels that
curve around
the stage I have created
to pleasure out this dance.

Commands are not living here
under the unseen Pleiades
in midday quiet.

VIII. Dans le quartier

I avoid that dark stand.

Globes of light curl around
the path I take.

Damp, black clothing is
bunched up on the grass.

I am attuned to avoid small stones, the ordure,
feel the pull
of a large rocky clump –
dive into that crevice
of overlapping spheres and triangles.

The fringed drapery of leaves
invites solitude.

I am at home in my calculations
and inquietude.

IX. Sur la montagne

Chamechaude

Peak upon peak.

Cool now,
I am left by the side of the road –
a few buildings
abandoned equipment
for grooming slopes
an old hotel and a new one
nothing more.

To wander down a red, muddy
logging road.
A short, steep climb over scree.

Signs of danger and pyres of
stone mark the way.

There is a steady caravan
curling up the mountain.
On attaining the quest, there is
a rock slide on one side
a sheer cliff on the other
that gives on
a soft-bushed valley and
roofs of a farm.

The many sheep and sleek
black goat
who were my companions
on this scramble, now
penned.

The blue-grey roofs over grey-white stone –
St. Hughes, St. Pierre, Le Grand Couvent.

I flutter and flap
in a blue poncho.

Shiny-headed crows
await and attack the crumbs
I scatter.

Have pushed harder
unremitting
since I am alone.

Found the cabled descent to the goat-path.

Disturbed a cabin-dweller and his silent dog
and passed on.

The coming and the going –
in a simple word – free.

Narrow and muddy, I slip into soft vegetation.
Then injure myself on the easy part of the path.

Hours of beer and observation
with women and the old,
drenched hikers with a kitten
in a sweater.

The abandoned hall –
dream of bed,
hot chocolate,
a book.

The sky cracks open –
in sun and shadow, I descend.

X. Dans le quartier

Blue-green light on a golden arc of urine.

My tired, lined face leaning by the curving path.

Bumped by college students
I stand fast.
This is my quarter
as much as anyone's
under these hunched mountains
which skulk against clouds
the rain not far off
but here –
clear, oh clear.

XI. *September*

A new shadow season
where green darkens and
movements are quenched.

There is red along the wall, thinning.

Happiness spouts in the midst of children
in my response is all the possibility of joy.

Now familiar, I hurry past –
the specific motion of lovers, and
the pillow warmth of bodies.

XII. Dans le quartier

Calm, slow movements
among the baby's cry.
Soft
cones
drop.
      Clouds
slip between stones.
The swallow chatter trembles.

Along the wall there is a thinning.

No one is here.

Alone in the hum
of this small place
I chose when it appeared large.

An upward thrust of green needles.

I lean out over the balcony
and the sea is infinitely far.

XIII. Sur la montagne

There is a randomness in this
memory of rupture,
festering release of bubbles
from the purulent
graceless past.
I see it reproduced before me
in this damaged child on the verge
of womanhood, and it does not seem
a fruitful arbour she enters.

The small girl in a plaid, pleated skirt,
white socks and black, shining shoes
is held by her mamie.
Ecstatic on the ramparts,
she could launch into the pure upper air
with her blazing face.

All around her smog and haze
curl their way to the peaks below.

On the edge today
I err.
A wrong turning veers
me away from the
groomed gardens
into the wild ones
and this is where I stay –

struck with memory.

XIV. Dans le quartier

I am coming from the other direction.
It is night – as silent as it will ever be here.

A clicking of bicycle wheels and voices sound.

In the morning I will stay tucked away.

Later, I will run through it –
simply another place
along the way.

XV. *November*

I am in the ice and leaf-hung air.
Scrawling vines with tiny red flames
deepen to scarlet and purple and brown
then disappear from the wall.
A splay-footed boy, his back against the wall.
A girl presses against him
blue and white, aghast in desire
above, below, beyond –
crushed kisses
moist tissues.
Ice patterns the grass
black, bare slants of trees.
Cold has set in. Slug
warmth curls at its centre.

XVI. Sur la montagne

With the imminent past
I walk up in cold
down in cold, with
sweat on my brow
remove coat, vest, scarf
make this nearly final effort
pass through
bedroom alcoves, piles of burnt
and unburnt trash
stench and fear.

I prepare an offering
if it is needed
try to keep my skull
from the stone.

I am surrounded now by
gold leaves shaking in the wind
the emptiness of the season.
A faraway ice-covered rock
pokes its face at me.
Not enough to quench the pink clarity
in this gravid morning of indulgences.
I blanch in the absent sun
the crystal-hung haze
filled with smoke.
My watch has stopped.

XVII. Dans le quartier

Muttering away, this is no way
to end my stay, and I notice
a grandmother – short, stout, cropped,
buttoned dress-coat, leading
a bundled child by the hand.

I peer down on the child's
round, trimmed hat, atop her
pink-coated body
as they pass.

I take my vantage now.
To one side, the alpine glow
in the evening sky.
A Magritte moon hung above it.
The Belledonne chain and its fresh snows.
To the other, street and traffic.
A cyclist pedals by.
A flood of students spews forth.

In front, still a pyramid
wonder at the oddly slanted trees.
Do they lean toward sun
or away from shadow?

Above, the bastille.

Beyond, a tree of gold.

Below, beer bottles and a carton.

Beyond, a white monument.

I think, aggressively:
This is *my* street, *my* sky
my home, and
walk on
at random.

XVIII. Dans le quartier

Human error –
Children are washed away.
Nothing moves.
Neither trams nor trains
except a slow
metal-beating protest
through garbage-filled streets.

I am well fed
in the midst of mourning.

XIX. Sur la montagne et dans le quartier

Chamrousse and Grenoble

My last day on this mountain
I am alone and pursued
by a shadow.

I have risen above the clouds away from
that distant wall of rock
and its habitations
my shelter for
a few months.

Nearly no one is here in
this deserted resort –
only a class of children almost
the same age as mine
French and English students.

At moments, everything
separates – moves away
from what I have imposed
and reclaims its own.

A solitary man
intervenes
in the sunset. We depart
back to a country
shaken by its
self-made crisis.
Now they quieten themselves
before Noël, stunned and timid.

The quarter is again just a
tram stop, a cold place
to rush past. A dark
pyramid, a lighted circle.

What I want receives me in
a few small rooms.

III

III

Singularity

I wandered into that abstract realm that held
                    and would not release me
An arc
       tangent
the rainbow angle deflects and scatters light
                 reverberates in the atmosphere
There is a dark side to a rainbow as well as to
                  the moon

A phase transition is a singularity in the complex plane

                  water to ice
                  helix to coil
                  plus to minus

a spring running under thin ice
a collapse of order or an initiation

a woman rising to compose herself
over a cup of coffee when the night before
she let fall each block of her body

a flip switch that occurs in the magnetic poles
         every two hundred thousand years
the shallow eutectic of energy

thoughts do not follow a
               mathematical order
      they climb their imaginary axis and take root
   illegally
joke with meaning – appear on the other
              side of the plane
without permission

So recently I stopped asking
         why you are
    not here anymore

Man on the moon

as well as in the moon.
I watched the televent
in a suffocating Texas classroom while
Neil Armstrong descended a ladder
onto a shiny surface in a
temperature-controlled suit
taking earth's atmosphere with him.

A rabbit in the moon but not on the moon –
lucky to be sucked up into that brilliance.
Soft foot stroking the cheek of my childhood.

Someone back in Mission Control
in a supercool room squawked *MCC here.*

Buzz followed next –
a real '50s name for a real '60s moment.
Michael Collins stayed above in orbit
not to be captivated by rock and dust.

Stolen silver brilliance again
in your departure gone
shunting moonlight through a vein
day eating up night
beside me on the pillowed now.

Maladaptive decadence

The male club-wings cannot have it both ways:
They cannot evolve simultaneously for the most efficient flight
and the most beautiful wing songs.
        —New York Times, May 5, 2017

high heels when running from the bear
climbing a mountain in a skirt
grizzly attacking the bear-proof garbage can
quetzal buried in the avocado tree
the club-winged manakin's solid wing bones
a bomb in the backpack monster trucks
search for the largest known prime
staying in bed all day while the snow falls
on the bed

grief and denial large abstract ideas
a headfirst dive into the truth
most of your DNA that encodes nothing
the biggest of anything – land mammal
sea mammal dinosaur
swimming on the edge of a vortex
beside a black hole space travel
                        (generally)

being the first of anything nearly always
guarantees you'll also be the last

Maxwell's Demon

Not a quasi-divine being,
but rather a *peculiar mode.*

Maxwell did not use
or like the term *daemon*
for this inimical violation,
called it only *a*
neat-fingered being.

Conservative believer,
yet open to new ideas,
Maxwell found himself
closed off from many
benefits of society.

Seeking control, he
invented the governor,
a useful device
for taking the train
to Cambridge
from Edinburgh
and back.

A young death.
A long legacy.

First to see particles
spin in the rings of Saturn.

His equations bind
electric and magnetic,
light cast in
partial differentials,
spidery fields.

Shut the door fast,
it's only a thought
experiment.

Negentropy or life –
a great unknowing.

Morning Meditation

Let's love today… the passing moment that will not come again.
       —James Schuyler

The infinite moment, in which we pendulum in eternal recurrence –
the oatmeal and apples and blueberries are not *exactly* those
I ate as a child with Alma and Manuel each morning
in the home of Mr. and Mrs. Gonzales but they curve
dangerously close to those cold and bitter mornings
like the figure-eight of time on an Etch A Sketch, each repetition
a hair away from the previous – a lovely Lissajous figure.

But those cherry blossoms assert today and a little wind
ruffles white petals while cars swish through the city.
I read *The Globe,* feed the cat, bathe, then swish through the city –
a moment in a life that will not come again.

Salt and Ashes

Fine sea salt sifts through my hands with the feel of ashes
in a cloisonné vase on my desk – cold metal waiting to be kissed
    when loneliness delivers peppery and smashed garlic sorrows.
Rosemary and thyme shadow a source burbling in
    the garden on an Aegean island abundant in grapes
    where I make a wine that has aged fourteen years, and continues to age,
to drink whenever the full moon slides into Virgo.
On a white cloth, I cut open cherry tomatoes, drizzle the most virgin olive oil,
    rest beside them slices of crusty, yeast-aerated bread, while I alternately roast
and cool my hide in the summer sun and water outside a hotel
    lost on the Finger Lakes near Aurora on this Gloomy Sunday.

Hand to mouth

I'd like to be better at forgiveness
not picking at that brittle broken nail
or hammering a rusty one into your
savage little heart –
nursing a grievance always feels
like feeding on my own skin
autopsy then autophagy
but that's my zombie midnight snack
light-headed I open my mouth
blood rushes out like the bloom of
a carnivorous flower

How is it possible to have compassion for myself?

Yellow leaves are blazing against the blue November sky
      not a new image but you probably don't know how rare that
blue is here in Vancouver
    in November

I'm an unskilled labourer in the field of life
      construction and deconstruction
tools slung over my shoulder

I hoist my belt high on the ladder rungs
            and hammer against the sky

hello eagle, heron, pelican
      will one of you lift me inside
    your incessant soaring?

Here in my pocket from the ocean a precious stone for you
      no home to return to

Dream Wedding

I stand here
in raw silk
not the first time
not the first dress

Thirty years ago
Toronto in March
synthetic chiffon
shifting against
Twenty-six-year-old body

Eight years later
in San Francisco
again
silk cream
brought back from China
tiny green and brown triangles
frog closures at the neck
slits up the side
different dress
different body
girl fetus attending

My husband alive
blown about
under a golden bridge
I totter on high heels

He wears a bow tie
says each of us
made our offering
to the wedding gods

The pregnancy
wanted for so long
almost makes him
believe in god
he says
almost
a sweet jest
not quite

Another wedding
girl child now a woman
Look in the mirror
nails broken and ragged

Hair undone
smeared makeup
muddy shoes
broken strap

Music starts
Is it time?

Who goes first?
friend? daughter?

I stagger down the aisle
Everyone stands

Forgive me
I miss you
What else
can I say
I do

In front of the *chuppah*
another man
with a witty remark
for the crowd

We swing dance
to "Ain't she sweet"

I look again
my dead husband

Aubade

Impossible not to think of the first dawn without you
and the reluctance of your leaving

There is a time in August when the year turns
and whispers of coolness in the morning

The height of the bed was higher than anything
I had ever climbed before I heaved my body across yours

I washed and oiled each limb, the torso
The delicate parts, the hands and feet

The coolness of your forehead matched the air
There was no wind sighing in the stillness

How could it be you were there and not there?

Today I can write the happiest song

after Pablo Neruda

Today I can write the happiest song.

Write "The sun is shining and wheels
itself through an endless sky."

The mist lifts itself from the horizon and sighs.

Today I can write the happiest song.
I loved him, and he loved me always.

Through days like this I held him in my arms.
He kissed me again and again under the endless sun.

Sometimes he loved me. I loved him too.
Was it possible not to love?

Today, I can write the happiest song
and know I have him no more, know he is gone.

See the finite sun, diminished in his absence,
write what rises from the soul like heat from the pavement,

know my love could not keep him and
the sun still glows whether he is here or not.

Someone is calling, close.
My reason accepts his absence.

My heart has found him and he is here with me.

The same sun draws shadows from the trees.
We, in this moment, are the same.

I love him, but uncertain, ask, how did I love him?
My voice has lost the way to his hearing.

He will never love another
as he did before my kisses.

His voice, his troubled body, his eyes now closed,
I love him, but am I certain? Maybe I no longer love him.

Love is so long, forgetting so soon.

A day like this one I held him as he died
and am satisfied even if I have lost him

though this is the last joy he gives me
these the only lines I ever write for him.

In my version of heaven

Alain is
lying
on one side
of me
and John
on the other
and on
each side
of them are
their earlier
wives
and lovers and
theirs next
to them
and there is
no jealousy
where we lie
with the
scattered
detritus
of a child's
colourful
band aid
torn corners
of potato chip
wrappers
discarded
Tosca flyers
but the day
is mild
and we laugh
all together
at those low
moans we made

in pleasure
or pain
and how
little
it all means
now

No thought, best thought

If there is no self
        do thoughts think themselves?

Some have asked if water
           remembers what was dissolved in it.

Those interrupted hydrogen bonds reconnect, wounded.

           But, no, water doesn't remember.

Is memory stored somewhere inside you
          or it is just a neural cascade?

There's a cost, you know, to erasing information.

I'm having trouble with this day.

         It's Sunday but without a child there's not much grace –
         just crackly interceptions and static transmissions.

Grace and mercy drop like the gentle rain, and there is no rain today.
Crab bisque, bus tickets, pillows warm from sleep. Gershwin, mercy, mercy, me.

Hymn to Life

It begins with a whoosh
in that amniotic rush
you know will knock
your lights out.

After a time
you start to expect it –
this thing life hits you
with a ton of bricks,
makes you think
so this is it
again.

Persuade you
in its coy way
there's one more card
up its sleeve,
one more spot for you
on its dance card,
and it is worth living
after all.

All the while coaxing you into its
arms for a death spiral and
crooning *love really is all*
it's cracked up to be.

You lie there in its arms
with crushed ribs and laboured breathing.
Is it ever enough?

You already know
sifting through dead letters
and dead leaves –
things that turn to mush
things that drift and flutter
things that don't,
even though it's snowing
the rarest of snows here
and it's your birthday.

Day of Atonement

I search for Kol Nidre
among the few words I know
in this language

Baruch atah adonai

What do I know
about you
grandfather

married once
one child
married a second time
two more

made hats
went broke
turned anarchist
threw bombs in theatres

Your image
passed down to me
with the punched cards
shuttled through the looms
of your last bitter years

None of this tells me
how you walked out of Poland
eighty years ago

or why your son wakes
after your death
seeking acceptance
in dreams and a life
of atonement

Final Blessing

I don't want you to suffer
because of me when I am gone

The traditional Jewish blessing of the dying
father to his eldest child –
Bless me too, Father, said Esau, bless me
                    too –

It was a kind wish
        a great
            late wish
a wish too late –

seeing a girl
with a desk lamp
rammed into her face
each hour of the night
and a woman
waking her
with accusations

See this girl
dropped off
at school one morning
told not to come home
unless she is going to change
(Change *how?*)

See this girl
trapped in a room, a car –
shouts and threats
        You'll be put in prison. You'll be committed

Where am I now she thought
if not in prison

This girl with welts on her body
struggling against suffocation with a pillow

A fifteen-year-old girl
standing in a phone booth
next to a 7-Eleven –
green and red Christmas colours –
hear her say
It's very bad. I need you to get me out of this

Yes, I know it's bad
You'll just have to tough it out
for a few more years

She became crafty
cautious
exploited what was there
sought the safety of friendship
        not kinship
became educated

did not ask for help again
though sometimes did receive it

Then she left this place of violence
for a new country
        a place where terrible things also happen

Yet I walked out one evening in the moonlight

a woman, unafraid

Day in lab, night in the cemetery

for Meg Torwl

Bright bubbling cells
everyone hopes to kill

The poor products of the body
go crazy
anti-apoptosing
like the pure products of America
Dr. Williams knew

Chemotherapy
like hammering a nail
into a board
over and over

until it can go no further

Running rituximab
through a convulsing body
Anything ending in "ab"
will cost you much more
than you want to pay

There's nothing more we can do now

I work in hell
the burning brightness of hell
the dark light of hell
where sequencing slides skim along
beneath the laser scan

Illumina named for
four bands of scintillating lights
pouring out in terabytes
from well upon well
no one gets to the bottom of them
no one is cured

Still searching
for the transcription factor grail
in the structure of the genome –

this four-colour map problem
not yet solved

The *wild type*
The unchanged one

The *mutant*
what survives

A change in order
and lung cancer thrives
My father turns to
ash in the ocean
born and dying in the serous sea
filmed with chlorinated effluents

For the longest time
my body would not create
not a baby
not a poem
And then it did
And now I wonder
what wild
unregulated creativity
will finally kill me

Legacy

A slide rule and a book
of mathematical tables.
The rule is made of bamboo,
flexible and smooth, it will not warp.

The inner plank and
glass lens slide easily
along self-lubricating grooves.
A case of cracked leather.

For 400 years mathematicians
and engineers used this device
based on the logarithms of John Napier,
known as Marvellous Merchiston.

Before I could read, I recited long
strings of Fibonacci numbers.
When I was eight, my father began
the lessons in set theory,

the critical distinction
between 'or' and 'and,'
union and intersection,
the empty set.

A poet asked me if my father
took his work home with him.
I don't think he knows many mathematicians.
Those who do understand

a mathematician *is* the work.
In this, like a poet.
The tables solve integrals
I no longer desire to.

The dead are finally forgiven

because roses bloom in November,
because they are exposed to the elements
announce themselves in the sweet smell of rot.
Because they have stood and now are fallen.
Because like small children they are not responsible.
Because they are without guile or deceit.
Because they are no longer strong or weak
      can hurt
      or be hurt.
The dead are finally forgiven
because no one remembers their names.

What is birth to change to death?

HD

In the beginning
the mother of all bombs
rains debris
from the heavens

Lees of dead
wine yeast
coat the bottom
of the barrel

There's a burr in the lamb's
wool on the day of resurrection
but no enchantment in Aries

The bread
in the oven
ready, coated
with dust
calls to the hungry

Sealed by fate
the holy sigil of
a body crushed
under the rubble –
scree we walk upon
like water

Last Light

I walk a double spiral made of ropes
  twigs
     mouse skeletons
guided by an electric candle's erratic flicker

where the first shall be last
     and the last
first

a random juggling

   of those who pass through one gate and out the next

     only to find themselves back where they started
in a celestial case of bush panic

I just walked round in a circle, didn't I ?
    they say
    trying to find a way out of the woods

getting nowhere before dark

asking *is this the day of the dead?*

Did I just pass this way once before?
      More than once?

Music meanders through the labyrinth
  seeking its key

I hear the call
  shooeee shush

There on the ground
    the key

Backbone of the Night

'The backbone of the night' is the Kalahari term for the Milky Way.

I grow thin in the dark matter
that torques the arms of the galaxy
and spews forth particles of light
like foam on the crest of an ocean wave.

I grow thin in Vancouver
surrounded by abundance
and on the streets of Bangkok
clogged with water and traffic.

I grow thin in Durban
with dust dogging my heels –
the crunch of my steps on gravel
like the sound of static from
the interstices of stars.

I grow thin in San Francisco
and New York from the exchange
of blood and secret yearnings.

I grow thin
in the jails of New Orleans
and Angola prison
from my own ignorance
and from others'.

I will grow thin
until the day comes
to lie on the ground
look up at the backbone of the night
and ask the earth to accept my geometry.

Ghost Poem

Ghosts are what went before.

We are ghost catchers.

I was at my uncle's shack by a lake full of water moccasins – slithery black
 snakes with yawning white mouths.

Water moccasins are ghosts of the stagnant water. They deliver the strange.

I remember visiting Emily Dickinson's house and seeing her white dress,
 her writing table and the stacks of poems she sewed together.

And she knew *who has not found the heaven below will fail of it above.*

Ghosts walk among us all the time and tread the fields of heaven.

I remember a drink called *Je ne regrette rien* that had champagne and
 calvados and lemon.

I did not regret drinking it.

Songs are living ghosts of the breath of the dead and can be intoxicating.

This is a poem about the last time you saw your mother.

I remember reading Raymond Queneau while sitting on the floor of an
 apartment in Toronto.

Zazie is still kicking ass in the Paris metro but someone has placed a bomb
 there to make more ghosts.

I remember a party with my roommates in Berkeley. I went to bed and
 one of the guests came crashing through the bedroom door, fell
 on top of me and passed out.

Being dead and being unconscious aren't as different as you might imagine.
    Only in one case the state is transient and you are still breathing.
    Ghosts breathe, too; in fact, they are breath.

I remember singing to my father before he died. *The eyes of Texas are upon*
    you all the live long day and I been workin' on the railroad.

I remember numb fingers on the flute. Football games and fights and fifths
    and freezing feet.

Wolverines love beaver meat more than anything else but you will never see
    one because they are ghost animals.

Sometimes they leave traces of hair high in the trees.

Beavers are benign animals engaged only in large engineering projects,
    symbols of the country I inhabit.

Sometimes I forget to remember, and that is when the trouble begins.
    You can't have opinions about facts. But you can certainly forget them.

Ghosts are the memories you forgot and the people you forgot to remember.

There was a day – a very bad day, he said, but only one day.

And now, next to the living, ghosts are the ones I love best
    – and sometimes most.

Author's Notes

"It's a blue day": Joanne Kyger (1934-2017) was a California poet associated with The Beat Generation and the San Francisco Renaissance. She lived for a time in Japan and was a student of Zen Buddhism.

In "The Devil," the quote at the beginning is a well-known Spanish proverb, which is translated in the last 2 lines.

In "The Last Days," the quote is from *Le Petit Prince* by Antoine de Saint-Exupéry and translates into English as "It is so mysterious, the country of tears."

"Today I can write the happiest song" is closely modelled on "Tonight I can write the saddest lines" by Pablo Neruda.

In "Day of Atonement," *Baruch atah adonai* means "Blessed art thou, O Lord," and opens many Hebrew prayers. The Kol Nidre is the special recitation for Yom Kippur – the Day of Atonement – and opens with the Aramaic words *Kol Nidre*, which mean "All vows."

In "Day in the lab, night in the cemetery," apoptosis refers to programmed cell death. Rituximab is an antibody-based drug therapy for lymphoma and other diseases. Illumina is a brand of DNA sequencer.

In "Ghost Poem," the quotation "who has not found the heaven below will fail of it above" is from a poem by Emily Dickinson. Zazie refers to the character in *Zazie dans le Métro* by Raymond Queneau.

The author wishes to thank the 2014 Seabeck Haiku Getaway in Washington State for the inspiration for the poem "Last Light."

Acknowledgements

I thank the editors of the following journals where earlier versions of a number of the poems in this book have appeared: *The Antigonish Review, Cider Press Review, ELQ/Exile, Event, The Maynard, Riddle Fence, Scrivener, The Toronto Quarterly, Popshot, Sow's Ear Review,* and *Vox Poetica.* I also thank the editors of the following anthologies: *Fracture, The Science of poetry/ The Poetry of science,* and *Sustenance: Writers from BC and Beyond on the Subject of Food.*

I am very grateful to my editor Garry Thomas Morse at Signature Editions for thoughtful comments on the poems. Evelyn Lau's unwavering encouragement and advice were critical for the development of the manuscript. Betsy Warland and Rachel Rose were mentors at the SFU Writer's Studio, and Betsy was especially helpful in the development of "Randonnées." Rhea Tregebov has offered time and again the gift of great poetic insight and knowledge of craft. Karen Solie at the Banff Centre Writing Studio helped me refine and polish the manuscript. Other poets who have inspired me in classes and workshops include Hoa Nguyen, Heather McHugh, Patrick Lane and Lorna Crozier. I thank, too, my writing group, The Adrift Collective.

My thanks also go out to the writer's retreat La Muse in France where I met Julie Baugnet with whom I collaborated on an artist's book. I am grateful to the Banff Centre, including the support there of the Audrey E. Klinck Scholarship Fund and the generosity of Patricia Klinck.

I thank Sara Blatt, Lil Blume, Gayle Raphanel, and Jane Munro for enduring friendship and support.

John, my love, you are often my first and best reader. You check my poems for scientific accuracy and give me love a thousand kisses deep. Your sharp intelligence and gentle touch are the pulse of my beating heart.

Ariel, thank you for the beauty of your being. Being able to share life and poetry and stories with you has meant everything to me. And lastly, merci à Alain, who was and is my constant companion, and who always knew.

Adrienne Drobnies has a doctorate in chemistry from the University of California at Berkeley; she has worked at Simon Fraser University and the Genome Sciences Centre in Vancouver. Her origins are in Texas and California and she has spent most of her life in Toronto and Vancouver. A graduate of the Simon Fraser University Writer's Studio, her poetry has appeared in Canadian literary magazines, including *The Antigonish Review, Event, Riddle Fence, The Toronto Quarterly*, and *The Maynard*, as well as *The Cider Press Review* and *Sow's Ear Review* in the US, and *Popshot Magazine* in the UK. She is an editor of a collection of poetry in French, *Poèmes sur Mesure*, by Alain Fournier. Her poetry received honourable mention in the Compton Poetry Prize and was shortlisted for the 2015 Vallum Award for poetry. Her long poem *"Randonnées"* won the Gwendolyn MacEwen Award for Best Suite of Poems by an Emerging Poet and was a finalist for the CBC literary award for poetry.